POCKET WISDOM SERIES

Renewal

Patience

Patience

A LITTLE BOOK OF

INNER STRENGTH

BY EKNATH EASWARAN

NILGIRI PRESS

The selections in this volume have been chosen
from the books and talks of Eknath Easwaran.

ISBN: 978-1-58638-045-8

Library of Congress Control Number: 2009936512

Printed on 100% postconsumer recycled paper

Publisher's Cataloging-in-Publication block
will be found on the last leaf of this book.

The Blue Mountain Center of Meditation publishes
books on how to lead a spiritual life in the home and
community. The Center also teaches Eknath Easwaran's
program of passage meditation at retreats.

TABLE OF CONTENTS

INTRODUCTION

PART ONE:

THE ORNAMENT OF THE BRAVE

PART TWO:

KINDNESS AT HOME & AT WORK

PART THREE:

PEACEMAKING

INTRODUCTION

PATIENCE IS THE ORNAMENT OF THE BRAVE

WHEN I WAS GROWING UP IN A LITTLE village in Kerala state, South India, my grandmother taught me more through her life than through words, but when anyone in the family needed a gentle correction, she always had a proverb ready. I often heard her repeat the beautiful phrase: "Patience is the ornament of the brave." Patience is the real badge of courage; it is equally the mark of love.

Being a good teacher takes patience; being a good doctor also takes patience. In fact, if you want to excel in anything, master any skill, patience is an asset. And if you want to love – your children, your parents, your partner, your colleagues – patience is an absolute necessity.

You may be dashing, glamorous, fascinating, and alluring; you may be tall, dark, and handsome; lissome and lovely – or whatever the current fancy may be. But without patience, you cannot be called a great lover; it would be a contradiction in terms.

"Well," most of us say, "I guess that leaves me out. Patience has never been my strong suit." Very, very few of us are born patient, especially today. There almost seems a conspiracy in our modern civilization to counsel just the opposite: be impatient, be angry, and "look out for number one." But what is life without patience? What use is money if we live in exasperation with those we love, if we cannot stand to live with our own family? What good is it to have your picture on the cover of *Time* if you cannot be patient with yourself?

"Patience is the ornament of the brave." What

a wonderful idea! Not swords or guns or medals, but patience. We seldom realize what power there is in patience. All the energy consumed in exploding against others, in retaliating, in unkind words, in the anger that brings grief to others and ulcers to ourselves – all that energy can be harnessed as positive, creative power, simply by learning patience.

PATIENCE COMES WITH PRACTICE

AFTER I GIVE A TALK, PEOPLE SOMETIMES come up to me and say, "But you don't know the atmosphere in my home! You haven't met my office mates!"

I hasten to assure them, "You don't have to give me the details. I wasn't raised in a cave." I grew up in a large extended family, where we couldn't escape rubbing shoulders with one another at every turn. Later I worked on campuses with thousands of students and attended hundreds of meetings where faculty members from all departments often disagreed, sometimes with passionate conviction. In every context there can be people who are difficult – every bit as difficult as we ourselves can be at times. Wherever we turn in life, we are liable to run into challenging predicaments.

When I was teaching on university campuses, however, I was also practicing meditation and trying to use the teachings of the mystics in my daily life. Gradually I learned to cease looking upon challenges as difficulties and began to see tense situations as opportunities to put my growing love to use. We can do this everywhere; the family context is perfect.

In every family, for example, there is likely to be somebody with a bit of Jonathan Swift in him. Swift, you know, had a sardonic tongue and a rather black sense of humor; he is said to have worn mourning on his birthday. This sort of thing has an inhibiting effect on everyone, and naturally enough, when the Jonathan of our own family enters the room, others may try to make themselves scarce. Not the person who is trying to take love seriously. She learns to come up with a genuine smile and say, "Come in, Jonathan! I've been looking forward to seeing you." To herself, she can add in a whisper, "I need the opportunity to deepen my patience."

This is a daily endeavor, like aerobic exercise. You don't stop exercising when your heart rate gets up to 85. You say, "My target rate is 120," and you keep at it until you get there. When your heart is accustomed to 120, you can start aiming for 130, then for 140. Where physical conditioning is concerned, everybody accepts this process.

It is exactly the same process for increasing patience. The resting rate for patience is zero. You say, "I don't have any patience at all. I blow my stack at the slightest provocation!" I commiserate with such people by patting them on the back and reminding them, "That is where everybody starts." With practice, when Jonathan goes out of his way to provoke you, you find you can bear it cheerfully for half an hour. With time, you reach the point where you can get through an entire Saturday morning without losing control. From seven-thirty until noon, you are so patient that you begin to relish your show of self-mastery. After lunch – wisely, I would say – you make yourself scarce again, because your patience has run dry. But if you keep at it with the same diligence in every arena of personal affairs, the great day arrives when you can be patient around poor Jonathan throughout the weekend. He does his level best to provoke you, but you say to yourself, "Oh, no, you don't! Those days are over. Nowadays I can be patience itself."

❧ TIMELESS WISDOM

THE TRUTHS I PLACE BEFORE YOU IN this little book of pocket wisdom are not my discoveries. They are based on the timeless wisdom of the great saints and sages who are the world's spiritual geniuses – men and women such as the Compassionate Buddha, Francis of Assisi, Teresa of Avila, and Mahatma Gandhi. Here you will also find stories I heard from my grandmother, who was the wisest person I have ever known. She was always aware of the Lord of Love within her, and within every person and creature around us in the beautiful village in Kerala, South India, where I grew up.

Many of Granny's stories were about Lord Krishna, who represents the spark of divinity in every heart, constantly calling us to return to him. In Indian mysticism, which has a genius for clothing the Infinite in human form, Krishna embodies the source of beauty and order in creation. His body is the dark blue of limitless space, and the galaxies hang from his neck like innumerable strands of jewels. His are the qualities that draw forth love: forgiveness, beauty, and a tender compassion for all creatures.

Even for a child, these stories about Krishna were a constant reminder that there is a spark of divinity – the Self – in everyone. It prompted us children to be a little more considerate, a little kinder, and a little more selfless with those around us.

BEING PATIENT WITH OURSELVES

JUST AS IT IS GOOD TO BE PATIENT WITH others, it is good to be patient with ourselves. We can all be haunted by our past mistakes, by the amount of time and energy we have wasted, but we must accept ourselves with all our strengths and weaknesses.

There are many obstacles in life, and they cannot be overcome unless we have infinite patience with ourselves. When we are patient with others, we cannot help being patient with ourselves.

Athletes, I understand, often keep a daily

record of their training. In the same spirit, I take a few minutes every evening to get a bird's-eye view of my day to see where I can improve.

This is not a negative survey. You are not finding fault with yourself. You are asking, "Where can I be a little more patient? Can I be a little more loving toward Amelia tomorrow? Can I be a little more helpful to John?" These are positive ways in which we can improve the quality of our daily living tomorrow in the light of what we have done today.

Because of our human conditioning, we all have a competitive instinct, which we can harness to compete not against others, but with ourselves. The question is not, "Can I be better than Harry?" but "Can I be better tomorrow than I was yesterday?"

Interestingly enough, this makes every day new. Tomorrow is never the same old day. There is always something more to be done: one or two steps to take on the path upward, some greater care to avoid the mistakes that all of us make in some small way. Instead of brooding over mistakes or feeling resigned to them, I would suggest taking every possible care not to repeat those mistakes tomorrow and making at least a little improvement in our daily behavior.

When you refrain from unkindness, you are uncovering your real nature. Unkindness is not really characteristic of anyone. Beneath the selfish conditioning that brings such sorrow to us and others is a core of goodness that is an essential part of the human personality. The behavior that covers this goodness is a mask, which we gradually remove in the course of spiritual growth. We don't have to make ourselves loving; we have only to remove unkindness from our speech and finally from our hearts.

 **PART ONE**

The Ornament of the Brave

LET NOTHING UPSET YOU

Let nothing upset you;
Let nothing frighten you.
Everything is changing;
God alone is changeless.
Patience attains the goal.
Who has God lacks nothing;
God alone fills every need.

— SAINT TERESA OF AVILA

❦ PATIENCE ATTAINS THE GOAL

SO INVERTED ARE OUR MODERN VALUES that we associate patience with passivity and admire those who bowl over their competitors in their rush to the top. The spiritual perspective turns this right side up. *"La paciencia todo lo alcanza,"* Saint Teresa used to repeat: patience attains everything. Through patience, every goal can be reached.

Teresa's language would have been a daring challenge to her brothers, who were conquistadors in the New World. For them, to conquer meant to impose their way on unsuspecting peoples through superior military might. But for Teresa the real battle was within, and the surest weapon against the negative forces in human consciousness is patience. Patience means self-mastery: the capacity to hold on and remain loving in a difficult situation when every atom of your being wants to turn and run.

FINDING SECURITY

WE SAW SOME CROCODILES IN THE AQUAR-ium the other day, and what impressed me most about them was their almost impenetrable armor. This is the kind of armor we have to develop in order to withstand the onslaught of life. To meet every challenge as it comes, we cannot allow vacillations in fortune and fame to affect us. One well-known actor has confessed that he chose to go into films to gain as much attention as possible, thinking he would find security. It was the one thing he did not find. Security is armor we must learn to put on *inside* of us. Every time we are patient in the face of agitation, every time we return forbearance for resentment, we strengthen this armor and deepen our security.

❂ WE HAVE THE CAPACITY TO CHOOSE

THE OTHER DAY I WAS STANDING WITH A friend watching our dog Muka watch a neighbor's cat. The cat, in turn, was watching a flock of birds. For a moment the scene was tranquil. Then the cat, being a cat, suddenly leaped at the birds. Almost at the same moment Muka, being a dog, leaped at the cat. And my friend leaped at Muka. That is exactly what happens in human affairs too. If someone is rude at work, we take it out on our partner at home, and he or she spreads irritation to everyone the next day. It not only happens with individuals; you can see nations behaving toward each other the same way.

I remember, many years ago, watching a man on television demonstrating a nuclear chain reaction. He stood in a room filled with mousetraps, each of which would release two table tennis balls when sprung. At the blackboard, he explained a little about uranium atoms being split by one neutron and releasing two. Then, without warning, he casually tossed a single table tennis ball into the traps. There was a *snap,* then a couple of other *snaps,* and in an instant, with a rattle like hail, the whole room was pelted with balls.

Without exaggeration, our globe is like that today. One person in a chronic state of anger spreads anger everywhere. When many people live in this state, continually on the edge of resentment, frustration, and hostility, the harvest is violence everywhere – in our hearts; our homes; our streets and cities; between estranged races, factions, and nations.

Detachment can break this chain reaction. A cat's instinct is to leap at birds; it has no choice. As a dog, Muka's instinct is to chase cats. But you and I are human; we have the capacity to choose our response. We can snap the chain of stimulus and response behavior by meeting resentment with patience, hatred with kindness, and fear with trust, in a sustained, consistent endeavor to staunch the spread of violence that threatens us all.

❧ GANDHI'S SANDALS

FREEING YOURSELF FROM INSTINCTIVE, reflex reactions will enrich all your relationships – even with those who oppose you. When you are kind to a foe, he ceases to be a foe. In time, he may even turn out to be a friend.

Gandhi's life was filled with such relationships. Once, during Gandhi's campaigns for the rights of Indians in South Africa, he came before the head of the Transvaal government, General Jan Smuts. Gandhi had already developed the essentials of his later style, and it is easy to picture him sitting before this able Boer soldier and informing him quietly: "I want you to know I intend to fight against your government."

Smuts must have thought he was hearing things. "You have come here to tell me that?" he laughs. "Is there anything more you want to say?"

"Yes," says Gandhi. "I am going to win."

Smuts is astonished. "Well," he says at last, "and how are you going to do this?"

Gandhi smiles. "With your help."

Years later Smuts admitted, not without humor, that this is exactly what Gandhi did. By his courage and by the inward toughness that allowed him to stick it out without yielding and without retaliation, Gandhi managed at last to win the general's respect and friendship. Indeed, in 1939, on Gandhi's seventieth birthday, Smuts returned a pair of sandals that Gandhi had made while imprisoned in South Africa and had given to him in 1914. "I have worn these sandals for many a summer since then," Smuts said, "even though I may feel that I am not worthy to stand in the shoes of so great a man."

KINDNESS IS STRENGTH

STRENGTH IS OFTEN EQUATED WITH THE capacity to attack, but to me it means the internal toughness to take whatever life deals out without losing your humanity. It is those who never stoop to retaliation, never demand an eye for an eye, who are truly strong. They have the toughness to be tender, even sweet, while resisting violence with all their heart. By contrast, those who are ready to strike back at the slightest provocation are not strong but fragile. They may espouse a higher view of human nature, but almost anything can break them and make them lash back at those they oppose.

When someone is being sarcastic or cruel to you, the natural response is to retaliate. If you want to be unshakeable, you have to train your mind in patience and endurance, the most grueling training that life offers. Life shows no mercy to those who lack this inner strength. Every virtue requires the toughness never to retreat in the face of challenge.

My grandmother had a very pungent phrase for difficult people: "A lash in the eye." We all know from experience how an eyelash in the eye can be so irritating that we just cannot think about anything else. That is exactly how difficult people affect those around them. But for the mystics, this lash in the eye is an opportunity for learning the skills in life that matter most: patience, forgiveness, and freedom from likes and dislikes. When they think of someone who has been a thorn in their flesh, they will say to themselves, "Without you, how could I ever have learned to be patient? How could I ever have learned to forgive?"

It is a very poor evaluation of human beings to think that impatience and violent reactions are part of human nature. We have to look to people like Mahatma Gandhi, who was kind under any provocation, to see what human nature is really like. Gandhi's life showed over and over that even a violent person will respond if exposed to someone who, by always being kind, focuses consistently on the highest in our nature.

🐧 SPEED – THE ENEMY OF PATIENCE

A FEW MONTHS AGO MY WIFE, CHRISTINE, and I drove to San Francisco for a movie. We got there early – one of my favorite ways of not being pressured by time – so, after we got our tickets, we decided to take a short walk. We were about to cross a busy street when a car stalled at the intersection next to us. The light turned green, and the driver of the car behind leaned on his horn. Nothing unusual; just another noisy incident in city life.

But the first driver did not simply sit and continue to crank his engine. In an instant, he had burst out of his car with a snarl and was trying to drag the other driver through the window. Before we realized what was happening, they were scuffling like animals.

Fortunately, a third party in the car intervened, and after more honking the intersection was cleared without injury. But if one of those men had had a gun, I realized, I might have witnessed not just a fight but a murder – all because of hurry, and the habit of getting excited when things don't go our way.

It shows how far we have traveled from patience when a few moments' delay, a trivial disappointment, an unexpected obstacle, makes someone explode in anger. Hurry makes a calm mind impossible, and without peace of mind, how can we enjoy anything, from a movie to good health? As for having things work out just how and when we want, wisdom demands that we learn to expect the unexpected. Life thinks nothing of making changes in our plans – after all, it has a lot of people in the picture. If we take personally every disruption of our schedule, we will go about feeling insecure most of the time.

🍎 PATIENCE ADDS TO HEALTH

PATIENCE IS NOT ONLY A MENTAL VIRTUE; it is an asset even for physical health. I'm sure you are aware of the way your heart races when you get impatient. Perhaps you have noticed, too, that your breathing becomes faster and shallower. Doesn't it seem reasonable that if you can strengthen your patience to such a degree that other people's behavior never upsets you, your heart, lungs, and nervous system will be on vacation? Don't take my word for it; try it. At first, I agree, you will feel some stress from going against an established habit. That is to be expected. After all, when you have been leading a sedentary life, walking only as far as the garage or the television set, it is stressful for a while to get out and jog; your heart and lungs complain. But how quickly they feel better for it! It is the same with patience; this is one of the grandest secrets of health.

Research today suggests that emotional immunity to negative states of mind may well be linked to physical immunity, even resistance to disease. A person who is even-minded, who doesn't get shaken if people speak ill of him or excited when they praise her to the skies – such a person, I submit, is a poor host for disease. That kind of inner toughness creates a protective buffer, an enhanced resistance to illness and the everyday stress of daily life.

THE FRAGRANCE OF GOODNESS

WHEN I WAS TEACHING ENGLISH AT A COLlege in central India, I remember, men leaving campus at the end of the day used to stop by the flower stand for garlands of jasmine to take home to the wives, mothers, and daughters in the family. Half a rupee, at that time, would buy a couple of feet of delicate petals with a haunting perfume.

Walking into my classes in those days was like entering a fragrant garden; so many girls had twisted garlands of ivory jasmine in their shining black hair. Some would do their hair in a style you may have seen in the frescoes from the Ajanta caves, with a bun on top, pulled a little to one side, and a garland woven around. Others had a little chignon at the back. But most of them simply twisted strings of blossoms into their long, thick braids. And even after the flowers had faded and been tossed away, the girls' hair would still be fragrant with the scent of jasmine. Certain boys used to sit at the back of class, sniff audibly, and heave sighs of appreciation.

Lovely flowers smell sweet, the Buddha says, but they fade, and their fragrance cannot last. The fragrance of goodness, however, abides. When you have been in the presence of someone who has love for all, you will take home with you a little of that person's kindness and patience, a heart at peace, just as the smell of roses remains in a room long after the flowers are gone. Even you and I, when we can forgive unkind words or malicious behavior and not carry agitation in our hearts, will leave a fragrance that others, too, will carry away.

◆ KIND OPPOSITION

AS WE GAIN SOME MASTERY IN THE PRAC-
tice of patience and kindness, interesting devel-
opments take place in the mind. Resentments
and hostilities that used to torment us will be
getting weaker; yet they will still be present. It is
a peculiar position. You find a little resentment,
a little sympathy – a curious mix.

For example, suppose somebody is rude to
you. You don't like the person, but you don't
dislike him, either – a great advance from your
previous attitude. You may feel hostile for a moment, but you know that hostility no longer
has the power to push you into doing or saying something you will regret. And because you
know you are in control, that experience will
leave no residue of resentment in your mind. I

don't mean you will like that person, not at first –
in fact, for five minutes or so you may positively
dislike him. But afterward you say to yourself,
"Oh, the fellow comes from a broken home, went
to a rough school, fell in with the wrong company; that's why he has become like that." Once
you know you can transform negative feelings in
this way, you have won a great victory.

Even so, you can't expect to sail through the
world in complete tranquility. When people criti-
cize you unfairly, you are not expected to say
"Thank you." When they denounce you, you're
not expected to praise them. Such responses
would be unnatural and unrealistic. We should
never connive at discourtesy or unkindness, for
others' sakes as well as for our own.

When someone is making a mistake or acting
unkindly, putting up tender opposition is often a
demonstration of just how much we care.

It is essential to oppose kindly, without withdrawing personal support, and not for the purpose of getting something we want or having our own way. And we must be prepared for the other person's irritation. Yet, after the initial displeasure, every sensitive person will realize that we care for him or her. In the long run, this will add respect and depth to our relationship.

❖ BEARING CHEERFULLY WITH LIFE

IN INDIA WE HAVE MANY NAMES FOR THE Lord and for the Divine Mother that remind us of his patience, her forgiveness. One such name is "He who bears with us and forgives us our mistakes."

This name encourages us, too, to be patient

and bear up cheerfully when life hands us something that we would rather not have to deal with. To judge by our responses to life's ordinary ups and downs, most of us say, "Give me only things I like. Don't give me anything I dislike; give it to Brian instead."

Even good people, when they have been struck down by illness or misfortune, sometimes ask, "Why did this happen to me?" This is a most peculiar question. What we should ask is, "Why should this happen to anybody?" Simply asking this question at a deeper level of awareness brings the patience to bear tragedies, releasing the insight and compassion to help others and to grow ourselves.

Pleasant and unpleasant together are the very texture of life. Only when we give our best, whatever comes – good or bad – can we live in freedom.

☙ THE LORD IS EVERYWHERE

MANY CENTURIES AGO IN INDIA, IN THE
state of Madras, lived an eminent mystic named
Andal. On one occasion she had spent the
night in the home of some devotees, and when
the women of the house came to wake her up,
they found Andal lying with her feet toward the
north. The housewives were shocked and con-
fused, for in some segments of Hindu society
the Lord is considered to dwell in the Himalayas
and pointing or touching with the feet is a sign
of disrespect. Andal replied only, "In what di-
rection shall I point my feet? If I point them to
the north, true, the Lord is there. But if I point
them to the south, is he not there? He is also in
the east and west. Shall I sleep standing on my
head?"

Similarly, there is nowhere we can go to leave

the Lord behind. At no time can we afford to lock ourselves in a closet and say, "He is not here, so I can be selfish. I can do whatever I like."

Often we are so concerned with the activities of the day, the little things that irritate us or the little pleasures we desire, that we lose our sense of proportion. Here the mystics try to remind us that "he who is everywhere" is not only enshrined in our heart; he pervades the entire cosmos.

ENDLESS RESOURCES

GREAT MYSTICS LIKE SAINT TERESA OR Mahatma Gandhi have broken through ordinary human limitations; their resources are immeasurable. The more they give, the more they have to give; the more they love, the more they are able to love.

Not only can you not exhaust such people; you find that they have given you so much patience that you, too, can pass it around a little more. "Here, Marilyn," they say, "let me give you a basketful of patience." "Hey, Rhett, you take two." They go about distributing patience, and their reservoir of love remains full. Even ordinary people like us will find that the more we keep on giving such gifts, the more we have to give.

Intellectually, this idea may be difficult to understand. The problem is our idea of the human being. We think we are very limited creatures, very small, good for maybe only fifteen minutes of love or patience before we crack. Instead of identifying with a higher image, we identify with a biochemical-mental organism. I don't spend much time trying to reason with this idea. I just say, try it for yourself: see how far you can stretch your patience.

Naturally, there will be lapses. But after a while, you will see for yourself how comfortable you feel with everybody, how secure you feel wherever you go. You will find that when you have to go into difficult situations, you will do so with a quiet sense of being equal to the challenge. You know you can listen to criticism calmly, keep your temper, and make your point with kindness and humor; and you know that, by and large, other people will respond.

Work, of course, offers plenty of such opportunities. But for most of us, the very best training ground is the home.

 PART TWO

Kindness at Home and at Work

THE WHOLE WORLD IS YOUR OWN

I tell you one thing –
If you want peace of mind,
    Do not find fault with others.

Rather learn to see your own faults.
Learn to make the whole world your own.

No one is a stranger, my child;
    This whole world is your own.

— SRI SARADA DEVI

If you want to draw near to God,

Seek him in the hearts of those around you.

Speak well of all, present or absent.

If you would be a light for others,

Be like the sun: show the same face to all.

To bring joy to a single heart is better

Than building countless shrines for worship;

To capture one heart through kindness is better

Than setting a thousand free.

This is the true lover of God,

Who lives with others,

Rises and eats and sleeps like others,

Gives and takes with others in the bazaar,

Yet never forgets God even for a moment.

— ABU SA'ID

◼ PATIENCE IN THE FAMILY

ONE OBVIOUS PLACE WE ALL DESIRE patience is with those who are not well. Grumbling, complaining, and suffering are part of being sick. It is a privilege to serve those who are in poor health and to put up cheerfully with an irritable remark.

Similarly, with older people. It is good to remember that old age will come to all, and when your body is not able to function well, the slightest effort can bring pain. At such times it is very difficult to be generous. Spiritual awareness teaches us to serve someone in this condition cheerfully and lovingly: it helps them, and it helps us grow as well.

Another place to learn patience is in taking care of small children. Infants, in particular, have no language except crying. They can't look at their watch and say, "It's half an hour past my mealtime, and I'm famished," or take their cereal off the shelf and eat. So they scream. That's their way of attracting attention, and if the response is not prompt, they scream louder and longer. It's not very easy to be patient and cheerful with a screaming baby on your hands; but that is just what makes it the perfect opportunity.

Nighttime, of course, is best of all. In India, where babies sometimes do not have a room of their own, nighttime can really be a problem. The baby will be in one corner of your room, the brother and sister in a second corner, a cousin who has come to the city for a job interview may be on the couch. And in the middle of the night your baby starts crying. Perhaps he has a stomach problem; perhaps he has an earache; maybe she just wants to play. After all, a baby doesn't see the logic of sleeping all night. "Here it is, one o'clock, and I'm wide awake. Why are all these people sleeping?" The little angel starts expressing the feelings of the moment, and everybody in the house gets upset.

At a time like this, we can remember the unity that binds everyone in the family into a whole. This is what spiritual living really means – its whole purpose is to strengthen us so that we can deal successfully with the trials of life, large and small.

THERE'S NO LIMIT

WHAT MAKES US IMPATIENT? THE MYSTICS give a good, scientific answer: acts of impatience, repeated over and over and over. Then how do we make ourselves more patient? By trying to be more patient every day. If we do everything we can every day to stretch our patience, one day it is going to be inexhaustible.

A few days ago, I was in the grocery store watching an exasperated young mother contend with her little one. Hitching a ride on the shopping cart, he seemed determined to throw in all the items advertised on television. Unfortunately, his fancies did not coincide with his mother's notions of nutrition. After she had taken half a dozen items out of the cart and set them back on the shelves, she announced for half the store to hear: "Patrick, there's a limit!"

Every parent can sympathize with her situation. But I wish I had been able to tell her something the mystics have proven to us with their very lives: there really is no limit to the patience we can develop.

◾ TAKING TIME TO LISTEN

THERE IS A PARADOX HIDDEN AT THE ROOT of our fast-paced lifestyle: the more time we try to save by hurrying, the less time we seem to have. In South India where I grew up, nobody tried to save time, yet we always had lots of it. One might almost say in the manner of Jesus, "Whosoever saves time shall lose it."

Everywhere today – on the freeways, in the stores, in our schools – the motto is faster, faster, faster, faster. We try to squeeze so much into our day that we end up with little time for anything – least of all, relationships. Being a good mother or father, brother or sister, friend or colleague, requires a lot of patience, and patience takes time.

One simple way to start deepening our relationships is to make it a point to listen carefully to our children or partner or neighbor every day. I listen with complete concentration to our children over meals, to their accounts of school, to what they will be doing on the weekend. This can take some patience, since children often give detailed and even fanciful accounts of their activities, but every minute we spend this way helps build an atmosphere of love that will protect them and us from the inevitable ups and downs of life.

THE WATER LILY

SOME OF THE MOST APPEALING NAMES FOR girls in India refer to flowers. In Central India, where the university draws students from every part of the country, my roll books carried regular garlands of tropical names. *Kumuda,* for example, is a lovely kind of water lily that the poets say blooms at night when the moon comes up. With such romantic associations, you can see why a girl named Kumuda would be faced with great expectations when she showed up as a freshman on a college campus.

Just as this beautiful lily waits for the moon to rise, the poets say, our heart is waiting for the love of the Lord to open it like a bud. When love of him begins to flood our heart, no discourteous word can come out of our mouth, no unkind act sully our hands, no jealous thought arise in our mind. This is when the human personality blossoms into full beauty.

When the lotus blooms, it doesn't need an advertising agency to generate name recognition. No one can keep away. Similarly, when you do your best to put other people first, even if it means ignoring your own private satisfactions, everybody enjoys being around you.

🐍 THE SNAKE WHO DIDN'T WANT TO PLAY

BEARING WITH PEOPLE, ESPECIALLY THOSE who really do cause us problems, is the essence of forgiveness. It is not particularly helpful to do this with a feeling of martyrdom, either; we need to bear with people cheerfully. This doesn't mean making ourselves into a doormat. Letting other people take undue advantage of us is not helpful to them any more than it is for us. Instead, we can bear with them and at the same time improve the situation with their help.

When it is necessary to show our love by

expressing disapproval, we should learn to disagree constructively. Sri Ramakrishna, a great saint of Bengal, advises us to hiss gently when necessary, but not to bite. This is particularly applicable in relationships with children, who can be ingenious in needling us to see how far they can go. What they are trying to say is, "Hiss at us so we'll know when to stop." I saw the value of a well-timed hiss when I was out for a walk with our dog Muka, who tries to play with every creature he sees. He found a snake in the garden and offered to play with it. The snake was doing whatever snakes do early in the morning, and when Muka tried to get it to play there was a sharp *hisss!* and Muka came hopping out of the grass like a jackrabbit.

HOUSEHOLDERS

I GREW UP LISTENING TO MY GRANNY'S stories, and I never grew tired of hearing these age-old tales again and again. I loved the ones about Sri Krishna, who is noted for a mischievous sense of fun. He is universally kind, always approachable, understanding, and serene. The imagery surrounding Krishna is of light and peace.

Krishna has a particularly warm corner in his heart for ordinary people who live in the world yet try to remember him. These are householder or lay devotees. They haven't left the world, as monastic devotees do; they keep their jobs and live right in the middle of family and society.

In the Hindu scriptures there is a story about a character named Narada, who is not a householder but a sort of immortal monk. Narada likes to travel about from ashram to ashram stirring people up with spiritual gossip: "In this ashram, three people attained illumination last week! In that ashram, they are meditating around the clock." Narada appears like this in many of our stories, and the consequences are always instructive.

Once, it is said, Narada asked Sri Krishna, "Why do you like these householders so much? They're not very regular in their practice. One moment they resolve to become very spiritual, and the next moment they forget all about it."

Sri Krishna pretended to think a while. "Narada," he said, "I want you to do something for me. Will you take this little oil lamp and carry it around the temple three times? Then I'll answer your question. But don't let the lamp go out."

As soon as Narada took the lamp outside,

Krishna called up the winds and said, "Now, blow!" Soon Narada felt hard-pressed. The north wind started blowing and the south wind started blowing, and there he was with this little oil lamp he couldn't let go out. But being illumined and immortal, he wasn't completely without resources. He held the lamp close and huddled over it to shield it from the wind, and somehow he managed to get around the temple three times with the flame still flickering. When he finally got back to Krishna, he was a little disheveled but still undaunted. "Well, Lord," he said, "here is the lamp."

Sri Krishna smiled. "Tell me, Narada, while you were going around the temple, how many times did you repeat my name?"

Narada hemmed and hawed. "With all this storm blowing, the north wind and the south wind ... actually ... I didn't really remember."

"Narada," Krishna said, "these householders have so many problems, the wind is blowing against them all the time. If they are able to remember me only a little part of the day, I am very pleased."

PATIENCE AT WORK

MANY DISAGREEMENTS DO NOT REALLY GO very deep. They are not settled by arguing. They are not solved through analysis and synthesis. They are resolved – or dissolved – through patience. Without patience, you start retaliating, and the other person gets more upset and retaliates too. Soon you have two people out of control. Instead, listen to what the other person is saying. How can you even answer if you do not listen? Refrain from answering immediately, and when you can, try a smile or a kind word; it can do so much to relax the atmosphere. Little by little, you can try a kind phrase, then a kind sentence. When you become really expert in love, you can throw in a kind subordinate clause.

This actually quiets the other person. Kind language is a sedative. When you answer harsh words or disrespect with kind words, you are writing a prescription and passing it to the other person: "Take this. It will keep your blood pressure down and calm your mind."

This is a vital skill, for whatever our role in life – student, teacher, doctor, parent, carpenter – we can't depend on people doing what we say in just the way we like. If you are a doctor, for example, you cannot expect to get patients who are well behaved, courteous, and prepared to carry out instructions cheerfully. You are going to get many whiny children and irritable adults. You will see people who are short-tem-pered, ask embarrassing questions, demand to see your diploma, and wouldn't dream of fol-lowing instructions they do not like. This is part of being a doctor. And every encounter is a les-son in love. When the nurse comes in and says, "You've got a real pill this time, doctor," you can say, "Terrific! I'm getting a lot of lessons today." Maybe the patient hasn't slept. He has been in pain for forty-eight hours, hasn't been able to eat his breakfast; do you expect him to be an angel? If you can be sympathetic, it may help as much as any medication. It is not only drugs or sur-gical procedures that help the sick. It's also the faith that you are not just doing a job for pay or for some personal research interest; you are concerned about his welfare.

✾ AN END TO LONELINESS

"ONCE YOU REALIZE THE SELF, THE divine core hidden in your own consciousness," the Upanishads say, "you will never be lonely again." Loneliness is epidemic today; even people with money and lofty social status can be stricken by this virus. Once we realize the Self, we don't have to beg, "Josie, please love me. Bernard, please be my friend." When the lotus blooms, Sri Ramakrishna reminds us, it has no need to say, "Bees, come to me"; they are already looking for blossoms. Similarly, when you discover the Self, you will find that you draw people to you naturally for inspiration, consolation, and strength.

By the same token, we can move closer to the Self by moving closer to other people. This is not always easy, especially at those times when we feel inclined to hole up inside ourselves. It is sometimes difficult, even exasperating, to work with others with different methods and ideas. As we learn to give and take and to pay more attention to the needs of others, however, security comes without our seeking it; we no longer feel isolated in a meaningless world.

When we live harmoniously with others, we do help them, but it is we who grow spiritually. When we avoid opportunities to work and live with others, we lose this precious opportunity for growth, which can come to us in no other way.

🐣 A PERFECT DAY

MOGUL ART, ONE OF THE HIGHLIGHTS OF artistic achievement in India, is often in miniature. The artist concentrated on very small areas, working with such tenderness and precision that one has to look carefully to see the love and labor that has gone into the image. Living is like Mogul art: the canvas is so small and the skill required so great that it's easy to overlook the potentialities for artistry and love.

One beautiful, balmy Sunday soon after my mother and nieces arrived from India, Christine and I took them out for ice cream. I rode in the back, with Meera on one side and Geetha on the other. They chatted gaily the whole way, without a break, asking me all kinds of questions. I kept reminding myself of what most of us older people forget: that every child has a point of view. They have their own way of looking at life, which makes them ask these questions, and for them things like why *Texaco* and *Mexico* should be spelled differently when the endings rhyme are matters of vital importance.

When we got to town, we had to walk slowly because my mother was almost eighty. The children, however, wanted to run – and they wanted me to join them. I didn't say, "It's not proper for a pompous professor to be running about. It takes away from his pomp." Instead, I made a good dash for it. I thought I would meet with appreciation, but little Geetha just objected, "You're not supposed to step on the lines." There was no "Thank you," no "Well done"; I had to do it all again.

Geetha was just learning to read, so when we reached the ice cream parlor she stood staring at the big board, examining each item. In India we usually have only two or three choices, so she was really baffled. "Uncle," she said, "What are all these flavors?"

She tried to read a few and then asked, "What is that long word I can't read?"

I said, "Pistachio."

"That's my flavor." So she got that, double dip, and Meera got Butter Brickle.

They nursed their cones all the way home. I was in the back seat between them again, and every now and then they would exchange licks – across my lap. My first impulse was to warn, "Don't drip on me!" Then I reminded myself that from their point of view ice cream is much more important than clothes. We made it home without incident, with the girls and my mother laughing happily about a perfect day.

We learn patience by practicing it, the Buddha says. What better way than by sharing time with children at their own pace and seeing life through their eyes?

A GARLAND OF WILDFLOWERS

KRISHNA IS OFTEN PORTRAYED AS A young man with a garland of wildflowers, the delicate blooms of the forest, around his neck. It's not a sophisticated corsage from the florist's shop; everything is natural, simple, beautiful.

The beauty and compelling attraction of this image is universal. Krishna is the spark of divinity in every heart, constantly calling us to return to him. As long as we are alienated from our real Self, we will be restless and unfulfilled, for this divine spark is our deepest nature, the innermost core of our being.

Indian poets have always been fond of the imagery of flowers. Meera, one of the most beloved saints of medieval India, tells Krishna in a song, "I am going to wear you like a flower in my hair, like earrings in my ears, like a garland around my neck, so that I remember you always." If we remember who is the source of all beauty, all plants will remind us of the Lord.

Houseplants are everywhere today; people have African violets on their desks at work, ferns on the TV, fig trees in the corner of the living room. In some places, it is fashionable to tear down a wall or open up a window and attach a miniature greenhouse. Why not do the same with patience and forgiveness? We can surround ourselves with compassion, open up our lives to goodwill. All these flourish with just a little care. When you fly off to Iceland on a tour, don't you ask your neighbor to take care of your African violets – spray them, chat with them, pick off the bugs? With the same attention, houseplants like love and tenderness will blossom in your life year-round.

Sri Krishna's garland of wildflowers is always fresh from the forest. When you or I receive flowers on a special occasion, we have difficulty keeping them fresh, but Krishna's garland never seems to fade. The Hindu scriptures say that this is a sure giveaway of a divine being. If you ever meet anyone whose corsage or buttonhole bloom never wilts, be alerted: this is no ordinary Joe or Jane!

❦ PEACEFUL SLEEP

MY MOTHER MUST HAVE BEEN BORN KIND; in seventy years I don't remember her uttering a hurtful word to anyone. But I was like everyone else. As children do, I sometimes said hurtful things that I was ashamed of afterward, and when I did, it would torment me. I would toss and turn throughout the night, and the next morning I would go straight to my cousin or whoever it was and say, "I hope what I said yesterday didn't hurt you." To make it worse, he would look at me blankly and ask, "What was it?"

I used to complain to my grandmother, "This isn't fair! He is the one who should feel hurt, and he doesn't even remember it. Why should I be the one who can't sleep?"

"That is the makings of what is in store for you," she would say mysteriously. "That is the way you learn." I didn't understand, and I could never get her to explain.

But she was right: my motivation grew. If somebody said something rude to me, I learned to hold back a rude response and think, "Oh, no. I don't want to lie awake at night!" That is how it began. Today that reversal has gone so far that if someone says or does something unkind to me I feel sorry for that person, not for myself.

🐘 BE KIND – BUT USE DISCRIMINATION

MY GRANDMOTHER WAS FOND OF A proverb: "Lack of discrimination is the source of the greatest danger." The capacity to know what should be done and what should not be done is called "discrimination," and it is one of life's most precious secrets.

In life, we will meet people with whom we have to be careful, using our discrimination. There are many situations in which we must proceed with caution.

In our Indian tradition we have countless stories to illustrate this, usually with a touch of homely humor. In one story, two boys, a bigger boy and a smaller boy, go to a sweetmeat shop to get two treats called *laddus,* which are very popular with children. They are extralarge laddus, so the bigger boy is carrying them. Suddenly, one treat falls and rolls into the gutter. The bigger boy tells the little fellow, "There goes your laddu!"

So the moral of the story is to be careful with such people. The little fellow should have sized up the situation and said, "I'll carry mine."

Another story is about a practical, down-to-earth spiritual teacher who has a young, tenderhearted disciple. After telling the disciple that everybody has a divine core, the teacher wants to see whether the young man has understood correctly. He sets him a simple test, telling the boy he wants a bucket from the bazaar.

Later that day, when the teacher brings hot water in the bucket for his bath, most of it just disappears. He calls to the boy, "Did you bring this bucket?"

"Yes."

"Where did you get it?"

"From one of the divinities in the bazaar."

"Oh, you got it from one of the gods in the bazaar?" the teacher asks with a smile. "Did you fill it with water?"

"No, I just trusted him."

The teacher says kindly, "You should have tested the bucket."

Similarly, if we go to the supermarket, there are certain things we must do. Always read the labels. Always check the price. Everywhere, a certain amount of care should be taken, a certain amount of responsibility should be assumed.

Exercising discrimination is part of being kind. We need to combine a soft heart with a hard nose.

"BE KIND, BE KIND, BE KIND"

THE GREAT MEDIEVAL MYSTIC JOHAN Ruysbroeck, when asked how to become perfect, gave the simple answer: "Be kind, be kind, be kind." When we remove all unkindness from our deeds, words, thoughts, and feelings, what remains is our natural state of love.

This may sound simple, but it demands many years of sustained effort to eliminate all unkindness from our inner and outer lives. Some would say that this is humanly impossible – that it is beyond human nature to return kindness for unkindness even in our thoughts. Only when we see someone who has attained these heights do we begin to say, "Maybe it is possible, after all." When we come in contact with such a person, we know there is no limit to our human capacity to love.

PART THREE

Peacemaking

Lord, make me an instrument of thy peace.

Where there is hatred, let me sow love;

Where there is injury, pardon;

Where there is doubt, faith;

Where there is despair, hope;

Where there is darkness, light;

Where there is sadness, joy.

O divine Master, grant that I may not
    so much seek

To be consoled as to console,

To be understood as to understand,

To be loved as to love;

For it is in giving that we receive;

It is in pardoning that we are pardoned;

It is in dying to self that we are

born to eternal life.

– SAINT FRANCIS OF ASSISI

ENJOYING THE DIFFERENCES

DIVERSITY IS A PART OF LIFE. IF ALL OF US thought and spoke and acted alike, the world would be about as interesting as a condominium with every room the same. Fortunately, we come from different homes, go to different schools, hold different jobs, and have been exposed to different influences. Naturally, when we get together in close relationships, we differ in all kinds of ways. If we are going to love, we have to accept difficult relationships; that is life. But this is not a matter for resignation. When you love, you live among difficulties not with resignation but with rejoicing.

The secret of this is profoundly simple: these differences amount to no more than one percent of who we are. We have ninety-nine percent in common. When all you see is the one percent of difference, life can be terribly difficult. But when you see the much larger whole, you will see that we all have the same fears, the same desires, the same hopes, the same human foibles. Instead of separating us, the one percent of superficial difference that remains makes up the drama of life.

When I came to the University of California on my first visit to this country, I remember going to a little store on Telegraph Avenue and asking for some half-and-half. In India we learned British English, of course, so I pronounced the words as the English do, with broad *a*'s, as in *father:* "ha'f and ha'f." The man just stared. "What?" I repeated myself: "I would like some half-and-half." He couldn't understand. Finally he went and got his wife, who fortunately was a little more patient. She brought me a little carton and explained, "You'll have to excuse my husband. You see, we say it 'haffen haff.'"

That is all the difference between us. Isn't there a song, "You say 'tomayto' and I say 'tomahto'; let's call the whole thing off"? That is all most quarrels amount to. If you can keep your eyes on what we have in common, you will find that most quarrels disappear.

You can anticipate other people's behavior and help them change it, too, if you only remember that the other person has feelings that are just as easily hurt as yours are. He, too, appreciates it when other people are kind. She, too, appreciates it when you are patient, even if she herself is irritating; in fact, she is ninety-nine percent you. Being with people who are different is not only unavoidable; it is a precious, vital necessity. Without the company of those who differ from us, we grow rigid and narrow-minded.

LISTENING WITH KINDNESS AND RESPECT

IN EVERY DISAGREEMENT – NOT ONLY IN THE home, but even at the international level – I would say it is really not ideological differences that divide people. It is lack of respect, which I would call lack of love. Most disagreements do not even require dialogue; all that is necessary is a set of flash cards. If Nick wants to make a point with Nora, he may have elaborate intellectual arguments to buttress his case, but while his mouth is talking away, his hand just brings out a big card and shows it to her: "I'm right." Then Nora flashes one of hers: "You're wrong!" You can use the same cards for all occasions, because that is all most quarrels amount to.

What provokes people in a quarrel is not so much facts or opinions, but the arrogance of these flash cards. Kindness here means the generous admission – not only with the tongue but also with the heart – that there is something in what you say, just as there is something in what I say. If I can listen to you with respect, it is usually only a short time before you listen with respect to me.

FINDING THE COMMON GROUND

FOR GANDHI, LOVE AND SELFLESS ACTION were one. "I don't want to be at home only with my friends," he said, "I want to be at home with my enemies too." It wasn't a matter of speaking; he lived it out through forty years of solid opposition.

The other day I saw some documentary

footage of Gandhi with a prominent political figure who opposed him so relentlessly that people said he had a problem for every solution Gandhi offered. These scenes were shot in 1944, when the two leaders met for a series of talks in which literally millions of lives were hanging in the balance. It took my breath away to see Gandhi treating his opponent with the affection one shows an intimate friend. At the beginning of each day's discussions, the man's face would be a mask of hostility; at the end of the day, both men would come out smiling and joking. Then, by the next morning, the man would have frozen over again, and Gandhi would start all over with the same cheerful patience, trying to find some common ground.

That is how the mystic approaches conflict, and it pulls the rug out from under all the traditional theories. There is a lot being written these days about conflict resolution, which I am glad to see. But no matter what you read, they will always say in effect, "This is how you deal with your opponent." Gandhi, Saint Francis, Saint Teresa would all say, "No. The moment you start thinking about the other person as an opponent, you make it impossible to find a solution." There are no opponents in a disagreement; there are simply two people facing a common problem. In other words, they are not in opposite camps. They are in the same camp: the real opponent is the problem.

To apply this, you have to set aside the question of who is to blame. We have a saying in my mother tongue: "It takes two to get married and two to quarrel." No matter what the circumstances, neither person bears sole responsibility for a quarrel. It is an encouraging outlook, because if both are responsible, both together can find a solution – not merely a compromise, but a way to resolve the quarrel peacefully.

To do this, it is necessary to listen – and listen with respect. For how can you end a quarrel if you do not even hear what the quarrel is about? How can you solve a problem with two sides if you never hear what the other side is? More than that, if you can't listen to the other person with detachment, you will not have the detachment to understand your own position objectively, either. It's not just one side of the problem you can't see; it's both. So listen with respect: it may hurt you, it may irritate you, but it is a healing process.

Gradually, if you can bear with this, you will find that you are no longer thinking about "my point of view" and "your point of view." Instead you say, "There is a point of view that is common to you *and* me, which we can discover together." Once you can do this, the quarrel is over. You may not have reached a solution – usually, in fact, there is a lot of hard work left to do. But the quarrel itself is over, because now you know that there are two of you playing on the same side against the problem.

🏵 UNITE AGAINST THE PROBLEM

YEARS AGO, I WATCHED THE BRAZILIAN athlete Pelé play his last game of soccer. He was retiring at the peak of his career, one of the best soccer players the world has seen, and in this last game he was playing with the New York Cosmos against a team for which he had scored his most memorable goals: Santos of Brazil. For the first half of the game, Pelé played his best for the Cosmos. But the second half had a brilliant touch: he joined his opponents and played his best for *them*. This is what we should do in a disagreement: play half the time for the other side, half the time for our own. It is not a question of sacrificing principles; this is the only way to see the whole.

If we could see the game more clearly – and the results were not so tragic – the spectacle of a quarrel would make us laugh. When we played soccer in my village, one of my cousins used to get so excited that he would shoot the ball into his own goal. We used to say, "Never mind the other side; watch out for Mandan." When two people quarrel, that's just what they are doing – scoring against their own side. Whatever the disagreement, *we* are the home team, the

Cosmos – all of us. Our problems, whether personal, national, or environmental, are the visitors. And the mystics say simply, "Support your team. There is the opponent, down at the other end of the field. Unite against the problem; don't go scrapping among yourselves."

Otherwise, there are no winners in this game. Once we divide against ourselves, whether at home or between races or nations, there can only be losers. On the other hand, there is no disagreement so serious that it cannot be set right if both sides can join hands and work hard for a common solution. It is not at all easy, and the results will not be immediate. But wherever there is hatred, complete love can be established; wherever there is conflict, complete unity can be established. The choice is up to us.

⬛ DEALING WITH DISLIKES

MY GRANNY HAD A DIRECT, DARING WAY of dealing with someone to whom one is allergic: try sitting down next to that person and starting up a pleasant conversation. You do not need to stay long; five casual minutes will do. It is the effort that counts. It may be painful at the time, but miraculously, over time, you are likely to find your allergy subsiding – not only with regard to that particular person, but also toward anybody who happens to be discourteous to you or who contradicts you. This simple skill will improve your health, your vitality, and ultimately even your physical appearance; for the mind in turmoil takes away from the beauty of our face, the beauty of our movements, the beauty of our voice, the beauty of our life.

On the other hand, always making yourself

the frame of reference – which is precisely what having strong likes and dislikes means – is comparable to spending the day being thrown like a Frisbee between conflicts. By evening you will be more tense than before and so exhausted that you cannot face the problems you have created for yourself. Instead of allowing the mind to spin its numberless wheels, it is in our own best interest to extend ourselves by working hard and giving as much time and energy as we can to other people. If you want a good friend, don't think about yourself. Be a good friend to all, think about the needs of everybody else, and you will be your own best friend.

☙ KIND ALWAYS

"LOVE SUFFERS LONG AND IS KIND," SAINT Paul says. This word – *kind* – is so simple that we seem to have forgotten what it means; it opens a great avenue of love.

Most of us can be kind under certain circumstances – at the right time, with the right people, in a certain place. Otherwise we simply stay away. We avoid someone, change jobs, leave home; if we have to, we move to Southern California. But as Jesus says, being kind when it is easy to be kind is not worthy of much applause. If we want to be kind always, we have to move closer to difficult people instead of moving away.

Thérèse of Lisieux, a charming saint of nineteenth-century France who died in her early twenties, was a great artist at this. In her convent, there was a senior nun whose manner Thérèse found offensive in every way. Like many of her sister nuns, I imagine, all that she wanted was to avoid this unfortunate woman. But Thérèse had daring. Where everyone else would slip away, she began to go out of her way to see this woman. She would speak kindly to her, sometimes bring her flowers, give her her best smile, and in general "do everything for her that I would do for someone I most love." Because of this love, the woman began to grow secure and to respond.

One day, in one of the most memorable scenes in Thérèse's autobiography, this other nun goes to Thérèse and asks, "Tell me, Sister, what is it about me that you find so appealing? You have such love in your smile when you see me, and your eyes shine with happiness." Her very image of herself has changed; for the first time in her life, perhaps, she has begun to think, "I must be a lovable woman!" That is the healing power of kindness.

⊞ TRUST IS A TWO-WAY STREET

WHAT WE ARE LOOKING FOR IN OTHERS is generally what we find. "Such as we are inwardly," Thomas à Kempis says, "so we judge outwardly." Psychology can go no deeper. When we ourselves are trustworthy, for example, we tend to see the same dependability in others – and when we do, interestingly enough, our trust is often rewarded, because trust is a two-way street. It is the same with our other judgments about life: it's amazing how quickly the world we live in conforms itself to our ideas about it.

You can test this intriguing law in the laboratory of your own life. If someone at work absolutely seems to enjoy making things rougher for you, try treating that person with extra respect – and go on showing him respect no matter how he acts. In a surprisingly short time, I predict, his behavior will begin to verify your faith in his better side.

This does not mean closing our eyes to wrong behavior. It means simply that we will never lose faith in any person's capacity to change. Without that faith, people lose faith in themselves, and without faith in yourself it is not possible to improve. Everyone deserves our respect, for all are children of a compassionate God. This is the most effective way to help others remember their true character.

❧ SEEING THE SELF IN ALL

THE INNER SELF IS PRESENT NOT ONLY IN those we like and who like us but equally in those we do not like and who dislike us. And when we attain spiritual awareness, we will see this reality in all, whether they are for us or against us, whether or not they belong to our race, sex, country, or religion.

To begin to see like this, we must learn to overcome our likes and dislikes. It is only natural to like those who like you, and to return dislike with dislike. We need a certain degree of detachment to be able to get along with people who are difficult – detachment not from them but from ourselves.

In English the word *detachment* sounds negative; people usually associate it with indifference. Actually, it is attachment to ourselves that makes us indifferent to others. What life requires is detachment from ourselves, which opens the door to sympathy, understanding, and compassion.

THE DOG WHO LIKED EVERYBODY

SOME TIME AGO, WHILE CHRISTINE WAS IN the bank, I decided to stay in the car and read the paper. The door of the car was open, and a dog, rather plebeian, came up and looked at me for a long time to see whether I would welcome a little company. He must have decided I would, because he put two paws on my lap and said, "Bowwow." I said, "Yes, thank you, I am always well." He had quite a nice way about him, so he probably would have understood if I had said instead, "I don't have time to talk to dogs"; I imagine he would have just said, "I feel sorry for you" and walked away. But I can understand the ways of dogs easily, and I started petting him. By this time he was drawing himself more and more into the car until at last more of him was in than out. He was sitting on my lap, and we were getting along very well when a woman who was passing by said jocularly, "He's a mutt. He likes everybody."

Mutt or not, I wanted to tell her, that dog was teaching us a lesson. Those who like everybody, even if their opinions or color or social status is different, have tremendous potential. Such people can go far spiritually, because they identify themselves very little with their body, their feelings, and their opinions. They do not forget that people are people just like them, so they do not put labels on them: "reactionary or radical," "straight or not so straight," "for me or against me." And they never make the mistake of thinking of people as political animals or economic units; for all of us have feelings that can be hurt and needs that should be respected. When you see someone like this, remind yourself that he or she already has some awareness that all of us are one.

🔲 LEARNING FORGIVENESS

EVEN TODAY, IN THIS AGE OF PRACTICAL psychology, at times we can be so insecure that without realizing it we may try to raise ourselves up by tearing somebody else down. When we get even a glimpse of the unity of life, we realize that in tearing others down we are tearing ourselves down too. Sitting in judgment on other people and countries and races is training your mind to sit in judgment on yourself. "Forgive us our trespasses as we forgive those who trespass against us." As we forgive others, we are teaching the mind to respond with forgiveness everywhere, even to the misdeeds and mistakes of our own past.

MADE IN HEAVEN

JESUS TAUGHT HIS DISCIPLES TO BEGIN their prayer with the words "Our Father." When we eliminate every trace of separateness from our hearts, we find ourselves united with one who is not only our Father but also, as we say in India, our Mother too.

This is not merely union but a reunion. Like the prodigal son, we have returned to the Lord after many years of wandering, to find the peace and security that can only elude us when we look for them outside ourselves. "There is no joy in the finite," the Upanishads say; "there is joy only in the infinite." Our capacity for joy is infinite, and anything less than infinitude can only leave us hungry and unfulfilled.

Meister Eckhart, the great German mystic, explains this vividly. All of us, he says, have the seed of God within us. Just as a farmer has to plant the seed, water it and nourish it, weed around it and protect it, so we have to develop our spiritual potential by systematic hard work. If we watch an apple tree over many seasons and see it producing thousands of apples, we can say that the potential for these apples was in the single seed from which that tree sprang. In the same way, we should remember that the God-seed is in all of us, waiting for the water and warmth and proper soil to quicken it into growth.

This makes everybody special. We all have a little label inside us that says, "Made in heaven." We may have almost rubbed it out; but if we look carefully, we can make out a few letters: "M– – – h – – ven." If we haven't quite made the best of our lives, it can be very reassuring to remember that nothing we or anyone else can do can take away this label of innate goodness. The point is that this label is in everyone. Everyone is special, because we are all the handiwork of the Lord.

PEACEMAKING

I FIRST CAME TO THE UNITED STATES IN 1959 by way of a P & O ocean liner, as part of the Fulbright exchange program. On board were several Fulbright scholars, including a few from countries whose relations with India were very strained. At the dining table they would take out their international frustrations on me as if I were the Prime Minister of India. I would plead innocence: "I am just a poor professor. What do I have to do with making important policies?" But my protests did little to stem the unpleasantness.

Quite a few of my Indian colleagues left the table to sit as far away as possible. I would have done the same before I had taken to meditation, but now I was secure. It is not that I did not understand the remarks. I understood them all too well, and I felt sad that neighboring countries should be indulging in such animosity. Yet it didn't really bother me except on their account. I simply didn't reply, but I didn't move away or become hostile, either.

The surprise ending came when I got off at Marseilles. These same hostile scholars came to see me. They were going on with the ship to Gibraltar, and they had decided to give me a farewell party. I was amazed and a little embarrassed when they said, "Please forgive us for whatever we said."

This is the natural human response to patience. There is no call to bury our heads in the sand and say, "Everybody is good; everybody is loving." We can acknowledge that the world is a difficult place but still have enough security, endurance, and love to remember that all these difficulties are only on the surface of life. Beneath the anger and agitation runs the river of love.

So the test of wisdom is your capacity to be friendly in the midst of differences and secure in the midst of opposition. This can be true of nations also. Einstein made the understatement of his career when he said, "We know a few things that the politicians do not know." I like that statement very much. When we lead, the politicians follow. Often we do not lead, so they mislead us.

THE FRAGRANCE OF THE HEART

AT WEDDINGS IN NORTH INDIA, IT IS CUStomary to apply distilled rose water to the wrist of each guest. It is so fragrant and lasts so long that wherever you go afterward people will smile and say, "Hey, you must have come from a wedding!" Just so, when you meet a lover of God, you take a little of that fragrance home in your heart. You will be more patient, more understanding, more secure, and more selfless.

That is why people loved to be around saints like Francis of Assisi and Teresa of Avila. We instinctively seek the company of men and women like this, and when we find them, we feel so comfortable – not even talking, just being nearby.

A kind of quietly healing influence can be felt

wherever there is even one person whose mind is at peace and whose heart is full of love.

🐦 THE JOY OF SAINT FRANCIS

THE MEDIEVAL MYSTIC FRANCIS OF ASSISI is perhaps the most universally loved of Christian saints. During his lifetime, his directness, humility, and uncontainable joy drew many to him to wander the roads of Italy. Today this joyful saint belongs to the whole world, and the stories of his brown-robed friars are told and retold. One of my favorites is about Francis and the faithful, steadfast Brother Leo.

One winter day, on a journey across the Italian countryside with Brother Leo, Saint Francis exclaims, "Brother Leo, even if all the friars were perfect examples of holiness, even if they taught and healed and performed all kinds of miracles, this would still not be perfect joy." Leo asks eagerly, "What is perfect joy?"

Francis, who knew how to make a point and how to tell a tale, replies, "Even if we could understand the birds, and speak with angels, and know all the secrets of nature – even then, Brother Leo, this would still not be perfect joy."

They walk along a little farther, with Francis going on and on like this, until finally Brother Leo gets lovingly exasperated. "Please tell me what perfect joy is!"

And Saint Francis tells him, "If we reach the next town by midnight tonight, cold and hungry and tired, and the gatekeeper tells us that we can't come in, that we are just a couple of ruffians, and he uses all kinds of bad Italian and beats us and drives us out – if we can remain patient and loving through all that, then we shall have perfect joy."

Imagine someone who cannot be disturbed even if you are rude or unkind to him. Imagine someone who moves closer to you when you get angry, instead of running away; someone who keeps showing respect even when you try to strike out and hurt him. Simply being around such a man or woman is a joy. Their patience rubs off. Gradually we want to be like that person. When we have a selfish impulse, we reject it; we have seen something higher. Once we have an ideal like this to live up to, we try to stretch ourselves a little every day, because we see opportunities in every challenge.

When you reach this stage, all boredom goes out of life. There is no time to feel unoccupied; all your waking moments are devoted to realizing who you are – who is the real Person who lives in this body of yours. You find choices everywhere: shall I live for myself, doing what pleases me even though it may not be very useful, or shall I give my time to helping others? As patience grows, you develop the capacity to make these choices in everything you do. Then you will find your spiritual growth swift and sure.

THE BLUE MOUNTAIN
CENTER OF MEDITATION

The Blue Mountain Center of Meditation publishes Easwaran's books, videos, and audios, and offers retreats on his eight-point program of passage meditation. For more information:

The Blue Mountain Center of Meditation
Box 256, Tomales, California 94971
Telephone: +1 707 878 2369
Toll-free in the US: 800 475 2369
Facsimile: +1 707 878 2375
Email: info@easwaran.org
www.easwaran.org

NILGIRI PRESS

TAKE YOUR TIME

Life today can feel so fragmented. Often we face enormous pressures both on the work front and at home. In *Take Your Time: How to Find Patience, Peace & Meaning*, Eknath Easwaran explains how, if we slow down, we can gain control over our minds and, gradually, over our lives as well.

Through anecdotes and insights, he shows how to try something different the next time we feel stressed and speeded up.

Step back, slow down, and find a doorway to joy and serenity where you might never have thought to look.

NILGIRI PRESS

THE BOOKS OF EKNATH EASWARAN

GANDHI THE MAN

Easwaran, who grew up in Gandhi's India, tells the story of the Mahatma's self-transformation from a shy, ineffective lawyer into a fearless, wise leader – showing how we, too, can transform anger into compassion, hatred into love.

"Comes closer to giving some sense of how Gandhi saw his life than any other account I have read."

– BILL MCKIBBEN, *New York Post*

NILGIRI PRESS

THE BOOKS OF EKNATH EASWARAN

PASSAGE MEDITATION

"This is the secret of meditation: we become what we meditate on." — EKNATH EASWARAN

This is an introduction to Easwaran's method of passage meditation, in which we choose inspirational texts, or passages, that embody our highest ideals and send them deep into consciousness through slow, sustained attention.

Passage Meditation offers a complete program to help us stay calm, kind, and focused at work and at home.

NILGIRI PRESS

THE BOOKS OF EKNATH EASWARAN

WORDS TO LIVE BY

Start your day – or end it – with this warmly encouraging collection of inspirational quotations for each day, accompanied by Easwaran's commentaries.

These quotes come from some of history's most brilliant philosophers, poets, and sages from all traditions. Easwaran takes these timeless truths and illustrates them with contemporary examples, showing how we can apply them in our own lives to face challenges with courage and compassion.

NILGIRI PRESS

STRENGTH IN THE STORM

We can't always control what life sends us, but we can choose how we respond. And that is mainly a matter of quieting the agitation in the mind. It's a simple idea, but one that goes deep – a truly calm mind can weather any storm.

And we learn to calm the mind through practice – there's no magic about it. This book offers insights, stories, practical techniques, and exercises that will help us release the wisdom we need to ride the waves of life minute by minute, day by day.

NILGIRI PRESS

RENEWAL

Our personal example is a powerful instrument of change, more powerful than we realize. *Renewal*, the first volume in Nilgiri Press's new Pocket Wisdom series, is a little book of hope, to lift our spirits and to offer surprising answers to the question, "But what can *I* do?"

With stories from India and the world's saints, gentle advice and penetrating insights, Easwaran shows how small daily efforts can add up to a powerful force for renewal.

NILGIRI PRESS

Eknath Easwaran (1910–1999) is respected around the world as an authentic teacher of timeless wisdom.

Born in a small village in Kerala state, India, Easwaran grew up listening to his grandmother's age-old stories, and learned from her wise, loving example as she guided and supported her busy extended family. As a young man, Easwaran visited Gandhi in his ashram and was deeply influenced by the way he brought spiritual values into daily life.

NILGIRI PRESS

Easwaran came to the United States on the Fulbright exchange program in 1959. In 1961 he founded the Blue Mountain Center of Meditation, which carries on his work today through publications and retreats. More than 1.5 million copies of his books are in print.

NILGIRI PRESS